WILL ROGERS
WIT *and* WISDOM

WILL ROGERS

As his best friends will always remember him.

WILL ROGERS
WIT *and* WISDOM

Compiled by

JACK LAIT

PICTORIAL EDITION
With Thirty-two Half-tone Illustrations

FREDERICK A. STOKES COMPANY
NEW YORK   MCMXXXVI

To

SHIRLEY TEMPLE

Will's fellow-worker and confidante,

who,

when she unveiled the plaque of him
in Hollywood's Rogers Memorial Hall,
drew the cord, faced the audience, and

said:

"I LOVED HIM, TOO!"

Foreword

Will Rogers had an overpowering horror of offending against those standards of stage, screen and radio which the trade classifies as "clean." He was famous for keeping his satire far from the borderlines of such transgression. When he starred in sophisticated Broadway revues, surrounded by demi-nudes and interlarded between risqué sketches and "blackouts," his material was never tainted with a suggestion of forbidden or disputable subjects in the realm of morality.

After he had become the ace of all amusement branches in which he had worked, he undertook to enter upon a new one—the "legitimate" drama. He accepted an engagement to tour the Pacific Coast centers in "Ah, Wilderness!" the Eugene O'Neill play in which George M. Cohan, another champion of unsullied entertainment, had starred in New York and the East for the Theatre Guild.

Rogers was eager to try his new stint, and eager to feel out the character, as he had agreed to make it his next film vehicle. He rehearsed with intense application, and though he continually predicted that he would be terrible in his first "straight" rôle, he played it with distinction and immediate success, submerging his powerful individuality in the character.

He was as tickled as a freshman who had made the football squad. He earned far less than he would have at any other of his regular activities, but he extended the tour to take in the smaller cities.

While appearing in Pasadena, he got a letter. It was from a minister, and it contained the following paragraph:

"Relying on you to give the public nothing that could bring the blush of shame to the cheek of a Christian, I attended your performance with my 14-year-old daughter. But, when you gave the scene in which the father visits his son in his bedroom and lectures him on the subject of relations with an immoral woman, I took my daughter by the hand and we left the theater. I have not been able to look her in the eyes since."

It was the most sudden and terrible shock of Will Rogers' life.

Never before had he received such a letter. His mail had mounted into the millions, not all favorable, of course, but not one message had ever taken him to task in this direction.

The scene referred to was one in which the country editor's son, crossed in his romance with a sweet girl, has gone "on the loose" for one evening, during which he drank too much and yielded to the crude advances of a beer-hall siren. After the boy has recovered from his hangover, the father lectures him rather mildly but effectively out of his own experience. The episode had never before been known to affect playgoers or critics at it did the Pasadena clergyman.

Rogers read it twice. Then he went to Henry Duffy, manager of the company, and said:

"I'm through. I could never again say those

lines—even to myself in the dark. If they hit one person—especially a minister—that way, I could never repeat them. The show is closed. And I won't do the picture, either."

Louis B. Mayer of Metro-Goldwyn-Mayer, who had borrowed Rogers for the part, was astonished when Rogers withdrew. Pleadings, arguments, were futile.

There was no other film in immediate preparation for Rogers.

So he decided he would take the flying vacation with his friend, Post, while a new script was being turned out.

They were both killed on that flight. That letter had cost him his life!

The quotations in this book from the writings, sayings and letters of America's beloved "poet-lariat" will not disclose a single word or thought which could jar the sensibilities of anyone, not even a Pasadena pastor.

He swung freely on his favorite topics—Congress, politics, international relations; he was biting, robust, colorful and blunt. But he was never salacious. Nor in his personal life did he ever tell a story or voice a line that his mother could not have heard. I know. He was my friend of a quarter of a century.

Many are the anecdotes of Will Rogers' beneficences. He gave vast sums to individual and organized charities, flew thousands of miles to drum up funds for sufferers from floods and other disasters, and "shelled out" with lavish hand always. He was especially free-handed with the cowboys and other ranch-hands who descended upon Hollywood to seek precarious livings in Western films, known in Hollywood as "hoss op'rys." He had been one of them; he was their idol, they were his flock.

The last Christmas that he lived to enjoy was spent on his ranch, where he found his only seclusion, where he could be with his family, and where he could ride and rope without an audience. The ranch was his jewel.

Mrs. Rogers had been hard put to select a

suitable Christmas gift for him that year. He had everything that he wanted. He never wore jewelry, his other tastes were homely and simple; so she struck an inspiration—a tractor.

Will was delighted with the tractor. It would be helpful. But the ground was hard and the new implement would not be in use until spring.

One morning, in early spring, Rogers' ranch foreman came to start the day and saw some seventy-five "cow-hands" gathered around the porch of the ranch-house. Soon Will came out. He drew the foreman aside and said:

"That plot over there, I want it plowed up and graded. So I've called in these boys for a few days' work."

The foreman looked surprised.

"But—boss," he said, "we've got the tractor."

"Yeh, I know," said Rogers. "But tractors don't have to eat."

Will Rogers and Dr. Nicholas Murray Butler, President of Columbia University, were great cronies, despite the disparity of their professions. The educator was one of Rogers' most consistent followers. Here is an anecdote in his own words:

"Will Rogers and I were great friends for many years and I could tell all sorts of anecdotes illustrative of his human qualities and his sense of humor. Here is one:

"Shortly before the November election of 1930 I went with a small group of friends to one of the theaters where Will was to give a characteristic performance as part of the program. We were seated some six or eight rows back from the stage and my seat was upon the aisle.

"In due time Will Rogers came in and with his familiar lariat and chewing-gum began to talk in characteristic fashion, meanwhile looking about the hall to see whether he recognized anyone upon whom he could crack a joke.

"His eye lighted upon me and he at once gave a most vigorous wink. I clenched my fist and shook it at him as a warning to turn his wit in some other direction. Pretty soon he winked again and then I knew we should not have long to wait.

"Then followed this from Will Rogers:

" 'There's a great friend of mine down there. I'm very fond of him. He's an awful nice fella. I first met him out in Oklahoma. You wouldn't think he'd ever been out in that country, but he has. I wish I could do something for him 'cause he's in awful trouble. But I can't think how to help him. There's terrible opposition to his re-election as Senator from Massachusetts because of the unpopularity he's stirred up by enforcin' the Prohibition Law in Philadelphia.'

"This was all he said. No name was mentioned. But as William M. Butler was a candidate for the Senate in Massachusetts and as Smedley D. Butler was filling the newspapers with ejaculations from Philadelphia, nothing more was needed."

Returning from Europe on the *Ile de France* with Will, we spent many hours deck-promenading and loafing, and he told me many characteristic little yarns which have never before seen print. One of them pictures colorfully

many of his outstanding characteristics. This
is about as he went on:

"There's a certain lady with British royal
c'nections who I met in Hollywood a few times.
I was in London, all by myself, later, and she
called me at the hotel, welcomed me to her
country, and invited me to dinner.

"Well, you know how I despise to put on a
tall hat and long tails, so I told her how I was
all messed up in business conf'rences and such,
but it would be nice if she'd come to the hotel
and have lunch with me.

"She said that'd be nice, and she'd meet me in
the lobby. She did, all right. She all but
knocked me outta the saddle. She had on a
leather aviation suit, red as a desert sunrise,
from boots to helmet, and she looked allfired
like a red devil. Anyway, I was stuck and I
headed with her towards the dinin' room, which
was crowded. Most ev'rybody knew her and
knew me, too.

"Bein' me, of course, I'd plumb forgot to
reserve a table. We stood there, stranded, in

the middle o' that big room. Ev'rybody stopped eatin' and old Bill was what you'd call perspirin' right down into his shoes. The head-waiter come a-runnin' and he fixed up a extry table— right in the center of it all.

"We sit. The lady orders a pitcher of ale, which she stowed away pronto, then went into Scotch-and-sodas with her vittels. She got to talkin' loud and louder, and the louder she talked the redder her outfit got, and the redder I got. Just as she got so she drowned out the rest of the whole room, comes a life-saver in Jo Davidson, my old friend, the sculptor. He came over and he mentioned a new bust he'd just finished, and he had it in his room. I jumped at the chance and said I'd drop in and see it. He excused hisself. I signed the check and out we paraded, ev'rybody lookin', open-mouthed.

"I asked where was Jo's room, and goldurn if it wasn't on the main floor, smack across from the dinin'-room door. Nothin' to do but go in, me and her, with the whole roomful of folks all lookin' at us. They didn' know it was Jo's room. They hadn't been a-watchin' him!

"Well, sir, there was so many Americans in that room, I knew right sure that item would get back across the ocean. So, soon's as I could get loose, I sot down and wrote Betty [Mrs. Rogers] and it was a tough letter to put down. Anyway, I assured her I was still all whole and she must disregard any gossip she might fall onto.

"Betty didn' take it wrong at all. And neither did Cal Coolidge and the Mrs., when I told them about it in the White House. Mrs. C., she laughed and had me to tell it all over again when some other guests come in."

WILL ROGERS

WILL HAD A FRIENDLY feud with all film writing-men, which he nursed and used as a standard *pièce de résistance* at gatherings of Hollywood professionals, though it was strictly in good fun.

His regular greeting to any scenario-scribbler on the lot always was:

"Hi, boy.   What you spoilin' now?"

Rogers and his pal, Shirley Temple, on the Fox Hollywood set. Rogers was the only professional that the management permitted to chum with Shirley because it seemed that they talked about the same language.

Cablegram Rush

Monte Carlo, Monaco,
June 22, '26.

President of U.S.
   White House

   Please send money. Unexpected
Diplomatic relations have sud-
denly arisen here which no one
could forsee. Please rush as
French taxi driver is waiting.
They are unusually impatient
when you owe them.

Willrog.

[4]

Will TOLD ME HOW
Franklin D. Roosevelt stumped him. He was
lunching with the President at the White House,
and the head of the nation said:

"Will, I've figured out a job for you. A good
job, a paying job and a patriotic job."

Will jerked his head up and countered:

"Now—none of those Cabinet jobs. You ain't
plannin' to fire some of the Brain Trust boys,
are you?"

"No. Nothing like that. This is a new job.
I'm going to appoint you to collect the foreign
war-debts—and pay you on a commission basis!"

Left to right, Jack Lait, author of this book, Bob Ripley, the famous creator of "Believe It or Not," and Will Rogers, aboard the *Ile de France* returning from abroad.

DURING HIS STAGE-run as the star of his last earthly endeavor, "Ah, Wilderness!" a rôle created by George M. Cohan, Will was called for a number of bows and a curtain speech at the end of every performance. He always ended his speech with:

"And I just wanna say to any of you good folks who've seen Georgie Cohan play the part I'm playin', you can go to the box-office and get your money back."

Nobody ever accepted his offer.

At a preview of one of his pictures, Will, who rarely enthused volubly, burst forth into typical Hollywood hyperbole, with such ejaculations as, "Marvelous!" "Stupendous!" The director was overjoyed and asked what particular element had evoked such unique outbursts, and Rogers said:

"It never happened before—why, I can understand what Stepin Fetchit is sayin'! Oughta retitle it 'Africa Speaks.'"

Getting an earful from Walter Winchell, the columnist who is supposed to have his own ear everywhere. They were both acting in Hollywood at the time.

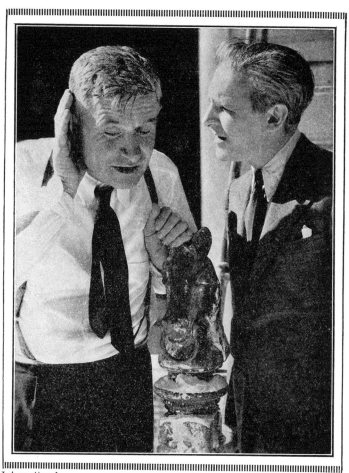

Will ROGERS, JR., after his father's death, bought a Beverly Hills newspaper; in fact, he bought two and merged them. The boy had always leaned toward a career in journalism. And Will once asked Amon Carter, the Fort Worth, Texas, publisher, to start junior as a cub.

Carter shortly thereafter wrote Will that he had a place open, and to send on the boy. Will wrote back, saying:

"If he takes the job, you better make arrangements with the local fire department to wake Will up every morning, or he'll never get to the office."

ONE OF THE COM-
paratively rare letters written and personally
signed by Rogers was addressed to Gerald Courtney, an attorney of Phoenix, Arizona. Courtney
was a candidate for office on the then risky side
of Prohibition repeal. The comedian, on the
air, had said, "Repeal is all right, but the wrong
people are for it." Courtney wrote him, asking
him where he got that opinion.

Rogers immediately dictated and signed what
for him was a lengthy reply, as follows:

Beverly Hills, Calif.

June 4th 1932

Dear Mr. Courtney:-

You sure hopped on me and took the hide off, but
you did it in such a nice and convincing way that you got me
believing it. I wasent stating a wish, I did think that all
that "society women collecting nickels" publicity, wouldent
aid the cause among the folks out in the country where its
got to be done in order to get it changed. Now may be I am
wrong about it but I think I know country folks pretty good
and I think Mrs. Astor and the society women taking nickels
for it would have the opposite effect, and as for the "wrong
people being for it to get it passed," why its the small
town preachers audience and your country folks that make
your laws, and they are the ones that you have to have to
get it changed, so thats what I meant by the wrong people,
if that crowd wanted it changed they could do it.

But my goodness I don't know anything about it,
and if you would look up any of my past writings you will
see that it was all against present prohibition, I have
lived off telling jokes on it for years, so you musent get
so touchy, I am no more a dry than a wet, I don't care what
happens to the thing, I am not going to waste my little
energy worrying over it.   Don't take what a comedian says
to heart, if anyone ever starts taking me serious I am sunk.
But again I want to thank you for your letter.   We don't
want to lose any sleep or friendship over what I say.   Drop
me a line and tell me you are not sore at me - gosh we have
all lost everything else we can't lose our friends.

Yours,

Will Rogers

Will Rogers as a minstrel man at a performance for the benefit of the Friars Club.

AFTER THE HISTORIC peace parley, where Woodrow Wilson magnanimously spurned all suggestions that the United States would take territory or other substantial payment for giving its men, billions and other monumental sacrifices for the freedom of mankind, Rogers dryly dropped a classic:

"Yep.   The United States never lost a war or won a conference."

WILL ROGERS' FIRST recorded wisecrack—though he was even then, while doing a silent Wild West "dumb act," known for his offstage wit among his fellow vaudevillians and circus performers—came at Tony Pastor's. He drew a round of applause at the end of his most difficult and intricate trick, wiped his forehead, and said in a barely audible stage-whisper:

"Spinnin' a rope is fun—if your neck ain't in it."

The best picture ever taken
of Will and Mrs. Rogers.
He is returning from a
trip around the world and
she has joined him for the
last lap in from Europe.

"ALL THE BIG WRITERS
nowadays are fetching out their books in volumes, or a series of volumes, rather. It's really the great American tragedy that it is being done that way. H. G. Wells has a new serial running in half a dozen sections with a warning that he can write a five-hundred-page postscript at a moment's notice.

"Theodore Dreiser got his hero in so bad in one volume that it took another bigger one to get him executed. The day of the 'one book man' is gone, the same as the day of the 'one gun man' in the movies was limited. The advantages of double-barrel over the old single-barrel breech-loading books is numerous. In the first place, you can always say in the second volume what you forgot to say (or hadent read probably) in the first book. Or, more handy still, you can use it for denial purposes. I hope to be like a good bookkeeper: when my volumes are finished my accusations and denials will balance so even that I haven't really said a thing."

His own Foreword to "Letters of a Self-made Diplomat":

"THESE ARE FACTS, and if there is a man connected in any way with them who dares to dispute them, let him rare up on his hind legs and proclaim it himself. I have always felt that a man can defend himself better than his remaining relatives. Then, besides, there was always the possibility of me passing out first."

Will Rogers and Eddie
Dowling opening a chil-
dren's playground in New
York's Ghetto.

WHEN SOME ONE called his attention to his ungrammatical use of the word "ain't":

"Maybe ain't ain't so correct, but I notice that lots of folks who ain't usin' ain't, ain't eatin'."

"ANY ONE CAN BE A Republican when the market is up, but when stocks is selling for no more than they're worth, I'll tell you, being a Republican is a sacrifice."

On war debts:

"I HAD A DEBT SCHEME that I told him of that I thought would have gotten us out with more money and more friendship than the course we have followed. It was this: Before anybody started to settle, why, let America agree on the lowest possible amount they could afford to take—that is, how much could they charge off. We will say, for example, we would be willing to take 50 cents on the dollar, at a small rate of interest and to be collected over a course of years. Then announce to the world our terms; all the same, no favorites. Nobody would have any kick about the other getting better terms. That's the way a business does—finds out what it can charge off and does it and has it over with."

In one of his last pictures, "Life Begins at 40," Will Rogers acting up with a sling-shot.

"I MUST TELL YOU about Venice. Say, what a fine swamp that Venice, Italy, turned out to be. I stepped out of the wrong side of a Venice taxicab and . . . they were three minutes fishing me out . . . I got seasick crossing an alley. . . . If you love to have some one row you in a boat you will love Venice. But don't try to walk or they will be searching for you with grappling hooks."

On getting a passport:

"WELL, I SAID I WOULD
like to get a passport to go to Europe. 'Here is
the application and here is an affadavit that
someone that we know will have to swear that
they know of your birth and you will have to
produce your Birth Certificate.'

"Well, I told her, 'Lady, I have no birth certificate; and as for someone here in New York
that was present at my birth and can swear to it,
I am afraid that will be rather difficult.'

" 'Haven't you somebody here that was there?'
she asked.

" 'You know the oldtime Ladies of which I am
a direct descendant. They were of a rather
modest and retiring nature, and being born was
rather a private affair, and not a public function.

" 'I have no one here in New York that wit-
nessed that historical event, and I doubt very
much if even in Oklahoma I could produce any
great amount of witnesses. My parents are dead;

Will, in Washington,
beaming with pride as he
greets his daughter, Mary,
and her leading man,
Myron McCormick, in her
first rôle as a professional
actress.

our old Family Doctor, bless his old heart, is no more. So what would you advise that I do? Will it be necessary for me to be born again, and just what procedure would you advise for me doing so? I remember Billy Sunday once remarking to us just before a collection that "we must be born again." I dident take it so literally until now. Billy had evidently been to Europe. You see, in the early days of the Indian Territory where I was born there was no such things as birth certificates. You being there was certificate enough. We generally took it for granted if you were there you must have at some time been born. In fact, that is about the only thing we dident dispute. While you were going through the trouble of getting a birth certificate you could be raising another child in that time.

" 'Having a certificate of being born was like wearing a raincoat in the water over a bathing-suit. I have no doubt if my folks had had the least premonition at my birth that I would some day wander beyond any further than a cow can stray, they would have made provisions for a proof of birth. The only place we ever had to get a passport for in those days was to go into Kansas. And I looked to have the average amount of intelligence of a child of my age and they knew that I would never want to go to Kansas.'

"Well, then the girl finally compromised by saying, 'Who here in New York knew your parents? We know you, Mr. Rogers, but it's a form that we have to go through with before you can get the passport. We have to have proof that you are an American citizen.'

"That was the first time I had ever been called on to prove that. Here my father and mother were both one-eighth Cherokee Indians and I have been on the Cherokee rolls since I was named, and my family had lived on one ranch for 75 years. But just offhand, how was I going to show that I was born in America? The English that I spoke had none of the earmarks of the Mayflower.

"I would have felt like going out without one

Left to right, Hal Roach, famous producer of film hokum, Harold Lloyd and Will Rogers, two of the world's most distinguished film comedians.

and trusting to luck to never get back again. So if you Foreigners think it is hard to get in here, you ain't seen nothing. You ought to be an American and try to get out once."

"WE CALL ROME THE seat of culture, but somebody stole the chair."

"Russian men wear their shirts hanging outside their pants. Well, any nation that don't know enough to stick their shirt-tail in will never get anywhere."

"Grammar and I get along like a Russian and a bathtub."

"COMMUNISM TO ME
is one-third practice and two-thirds explanation."

"Stalin—the Borah of the Black Sea."

Discussing Trotsky:
"I just wanted to see did he eat, drink, sleep, laugh and act human, or was his whole life taken up for the betterment of mankind."

An early photo of Will
taken in his vaudeville
days, when he was lost
without his lariat and his
leather pants.

"THEY ALL SAID TO me, 'Oh, no, Will! The better element are all against him.' Well, I knew that, but I also knew Pennsylvania. There are very few of the better element in Pennsylvania. I don't know offhand of a State, according to its population, that has fewer better element. Of course I hope that nothing disastrous turns out, but I warned them three months ago to procure more better element."

"I WAS GONNA WRITE a book about the war, but I heard some fellow had already done it."

"There's nothing as useless—outside of a Rogers closeup—as a convention."

"I don't know what the late war in Europe was about, but the scrap in the Far East was the first war over beans that I know about—soy beans."

Following his confinement in a hospital after an operation for appendicitis:
"People couldn't have been any nicer to me if I had died."

Back in 1925, when Will
taught Will, Jr., how to
spin the rope which started
him to the status of a
world-wide celebrity and
millionaire.

Will Rogers

Opposing Prohibition:

"IF WE MUST SIN, let's sin quick and don't let it be a long, lingering sinning."

Returning from a European trip:

"I am bringing family greetings from Dublin to every man on the force."

"I tried to find out who the Barbarians were. From the best I could learn, Barbarians were people who stole from you. If you stole from the Barbarians you were indexed in your history as a Christian."

In a dispatch from Nice, France, Rogers appended this explanation:

"I<small>T'S</small> PRONOUNCED neece, not nice; they have no word for nice in French."

"A<small>RGENTINA</small> EXPORTS wheat, meat and gigolos, and the United States puts a tariff on the wrong two."

Back in 1922, when Will
Rogers was a comedian in
silent pictures, and, by the
way, a distinct failure. This
shot is from "The Head-
less Horseman."

"I<small>F A MAN HASENT</small> made a success out of his own business we don't want him practising on ours. The cheap man is the high-priced man in the finish, it's not what you pay a man to go in, it's what he has cost you after he gets in that we have to look out for.

"We got a lot of Senators in there that have been elected on nothing but a Slogan, but what have they cost us after they got in? You see, it ain't the initial cost of a Senator that we have to look out for, it's his upkeep after we get him in there. He may be the deciding vote on one appropriation bill that will cost the country more than a hundred high-priced men would. You take a fellow that has never juggled with real jack and he don't know the value of it, a billion and a million sound so much alike that he thinks all the difference is just in the spelling.

"You see, with a cheap guy in there the voters never get a penny out of the election, and nobody gets anything, so I am a strong advocate for selling the seats to the highest bidder; they do it on the Stock Exchange and it has proved successful, and I don't see why we can't do it with the Senate seats."

Will Rogers and Wiley Post in Seattle, halfway to doom and death which awaited them in Alaska on their last joint flight, looking up at the flying ceiling.

"THE SENATE IS JUST a club that ninety-six men belong to, and pay no dues.

"Now, you can't run that cheap a club and make it pay; I tell you the day has passed in America when the successful candidate can go about bragging on the fact that he "was elected on $22.45 worth of 5-cent cigars." We don't want that type of man; if he is not a big enough man to hand out over a nickel cigar he is not a big enough man to run the biggest business in the world. Besides we don't want men in there who would represent voters that smoked 5-cent cigars. No man is any better than his constituency, and if nickel voters elected him he is a nickel man at heart. I want to see the day come when the least a vote will sell for is a Ford Car, and not a Henry Clay Cigar. If we can't be a good nation, let's at least not be accused of being a cheap nation."

"THE REPUBLICANS have a habit of having three bad years and one good one, and the good one always happens to be election year."

"WE ARE A NATION that runs in spite of and not on account of our Government."

"THE MONGOLIANS attacked and absorbed China until the supply of Mongolians gave out."

Will Rogers at the track in
Miami, with Gene Sarazen,
the golfer.

Will Rogers

On meeting Edward VIII (then Prince of Wales):

"ONE THING THAT I want you to know that will establish his character better than anything else and show you that he has a real sense of humor is when I first come in I said, 'Hello, old-timer! How are you falling these days?' and he replied as quick as a flash, 'All over the place. I got my shoulder broke since I saw you last.'

"I said, 'We will have to get you better jumping horses that don't fall.'

"He started in right away defending the horses he had ridden: 'Oh, they were very splendid horses; they were just unfortunate in falling, that's all.'"

"DO YOU KNOW, AS a real matter of fact, that Criminal Statistics of England prove that in all the murders that have been committed here [England], over 50 per cent of the ones that committed the crime have committed suicide before or right after being caught? They do that rather than face the law. They know that they will be caught, and they know what will happen to them after they are caught. So rather than face it they kill themselves. Can you imagine a fellow in some big city over home committing suicide for fear he would be caught, or funnier still one committing suicide for fear of what would happen to him after he did get caught? It wouldn't be possible for an American criminal to commit suicide. It would require too big a sense of humor."

Though Will Rogers' marriage was one of the most perfect and serene and devoted in theatrical history, he and his wife were rarely seen together in public. Here is one time when they were watching the Olympic Games in Los Angeles.

Will as a linotype operator
in a film scene.

Will Rogers

How to get rid of excess cotton:

"LET EVERYBODY put it in their ears to keep from hearing campaign speeches."

"I MIGHT HAVE GONE to West Point but I was too proud to speak to a Congressman."

"DURING A DULL moment Mrs. Morrow was telling me what an awful fine son-in-law Lindbergh had turned out to be, said you'd be surprised how he had reformed and settled down, said that some days he wouldn't fly over 500 miles."

"YOU SHOULD SEE Pompeii. Philadelphia comes nearer approaching it than any big city I know of."

Will Rogers speaking at a
luncheon to raise funds for
charity.

On meeting Mussolini:

"Everybody in the world had either flew to the North Pole this summer or was trying to see Mussolini. Well, I took the Mussolini end, because there are two Poles but only one Mussolini.

"So I says, 'Benito'—that's his Christian name, and in Spanish means pretty. That is the only false alarm I found him sailing under. He was not what I would term pretty. He was cute, but not pretty. Well, I says, 'Come on, Claremore, les see what Rome has got.'

"Well, I come in a-grinning. I thought he has got to be a pretty tough guy if he don't grin with you. Well, he did, and he got up and come out and met us at about the 4th green, shook hands smiling, and asked in English, 'Interview?' I said 'No interview.' Well, that certainly did make the hit with him; he was standing facing me, and he put both hands on my shoulders and said, 'Hurray! Bravo! No interview!'

" 'You hold a lot of different jobs here'—you know, he is the McAdoo of Italy for running everything—'you are Minister of—' He interrupted me, and laughingly counted off on his fingers, 'Me—one, two, three, four, five, six—Me, Six Ministers,' and laughed as he told me. He had sense of humor enough to realize what an outsider would think of one man holding six so-prominent positions.

"You know, I have, and of course you have heard about this terrible stomach trouble he is supposed to have. And then, I have, on just as good authority, heard it denied. We often speak of a man's stomach in regard to his amount of nerve. Well, if that's any sign of a stomach I would like to trade him mine for his, and there has never been nothing the matter with mine outside of nerve. If it's a bad stomach that is doing all this in Italy, why, what the world needs right now is more bad stomachs. Even just a little biliousness would help France.

With the Ziegfeld's—at the laying of the cornerstone of the Ziegfeld Theatre in New York. Will Rogers, Billie Burke Ziegfeld, Patricia Burke Ziegfeld and the great Ziegfeld himself.

"'Signor Rogers, Compliments, Mussolini,' and then the date, as he was proud that the picture had been taken that very morning; so he put the place and date. It was a horse—and him accompanying him—making a jump; not a high jump particularly, but a good jump for Six Ministers to make at once."

"I KNOW ENGLISHMEN
that have had the same well-bred butler all their
lives and they are just as rude as they ever were."

When introduced at a bankers' convention:

"GENTLEMEN, YOU
are as fine a group of men as ever foreclosed a
mortgage on a widow. I'm glad to be with you
shylocks."

With Mickey Rooney, the rising young film performer. Will Rogers is taking in the youngster's earnest palaver with open mouth and closed eyes.

"THERE AIN'T BUT one word wrong with every one of us in the world, and that's selfishness."

"EXPLAINING RUSSIA is just like explaining the NRA. I read a book called 'The Heart of Russia.' Now, suppose someone tried to write a book about the Heart of America. Maine's gone Democratic and California's gone nuts. Now, if you couldn't tell about America, how are you going to do it about Russia, a country that's so much bigger than ours that we'd rattle around inside of it like an idea in Congress?"

"THEY SAY CHILDREN in kindergarten must play in order to get them to learn. What do you mean, children? Crossword puzzles learned grown folks more words than school-teachers. And what arithmetic the women folks know they got at a bridge table. Our splendid English comes from attending the movies. Yes, sir, there is 120 million in the American kindergarten."

Will in an informal, personal picture, one of the rare instances when he had a serious expression.

Will Rogers

How to get a number on a dial telephone:

"WHEN I WANT A
number I just call my wife.   Then she calls one
of our children.   After that my wife and I stand
around and give advice while the kid does the
work.   It's all automatic, you know."

After Haile Selassie's vain plea for League intervention in the Italo-Ethiopian war:

"I WONDER IF THIS Abyssinian king could sue and get his dues that he has paid into the League of Nations for protection."

"ANY MAN THAT knows enough to say nothing always wins the admiration of those of us who feel that we can do the talking much better than he can, anyway. It takes a smart man to differ with me."

Rogers in a domestic comedy scene from one of his first sound pictures.

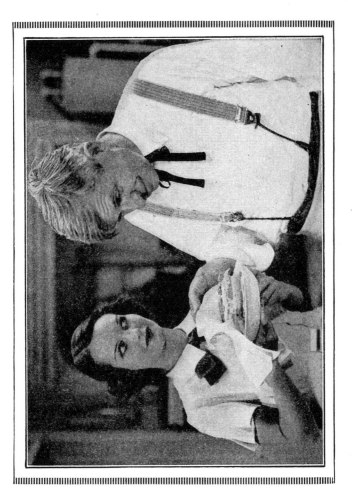

Farm Problem in England:

"And by the way there is no Farm Relief problem over here [England]. This is only a suggestion and I doubt if it could be carried out, but I think some work on those farms over home wouldent be a bad solution to their problem. These fellows looked like they had solved their farm problems by working on them. I won't be certain, but I think that's it.

"You see, they have figured out the jimson-weeds and cockleburs and sunflowers and all kinds of weeds take up as much room and as much nourishment out of the ground as wheat or oats do, so they just don't raise them. They will pull 'em out with their hands if they have to. The trouble with our farmers is that they raise too many things they can't sell. These only raise what they plant there to raise. But they ought to raise more over here; they have more time. They don't drive to town till they drive in to sell something. Gloria Swanson proving that virtue will triumph in the end is taken as a matter of fact. They don't have to go every night to see it proved. Leaving the field and going to a Lions' Luncheon is another thing they have never figured as an actual farmers' accomplishment toward less weeds and more porridge.

"Just imagine! I was in a farmer's house here and he and his family had a book instead of a radio."

Will Rogers clowning him-
self as a writer. His "pieces"
were always short, but here
he is working on about a
ream of copy-paper.

Will Rogers

On the British General Strike:

"But if you are going to do a strike over home you either do it or don't do it; don't advertise it and then not go through with it. If you bill anything as such in the papers over there you got to put it on. So all I blame England for was the billing. It should have been called A Temporary Cessation of Employment Without Monetary Consideration for an Indefinite Period, Without Animosity or Hostile Design."

"Now France wants
to get in on the debt settlement. On account of
them paying nothing, as it is, under the new
settlement we are to start paying them."

*President Coolidge was reported worrying
over the state of the nation.*

"I never knew a
Vermonter to do any tremendous worrying on
$75,000 a year."

Next to flying, Will Rogers' abiding passion was polo, and he played a stiff game. This pose is at Meadowbrook, Long Island, where he was in the national finals.

"IN HOLLYWOOD THE woods are full of people that learned to write, but evidently can't read. If they could read their stuff they'd stop writing."

"RUSSIANS MAKE mighty good husbands. If their wives raise anything, why, the husbands are perfectly willing to take it to town, and sell it."

"A BUNCH OF AMERIcan tourists were hissed and stoned yesterday in France, but not until they had finished buying."

Special Cable:

CALCOOL, Whitehousewash:

LONDON: May 18.--You can pick an American bootlegger out of a crowd of Americans every time. He will be the one that is sober.

Yours temperately,

WILLROG.

At Palm Beach, Will Rogers and Al Smith, Jr., son of the then Governor of New York State.

"IT IS OPEN SEASON now in Europe for grouse and Americans; they shoot the grouse to put them out of their misery."

"I'M ENTIRELY DIF- ferent from the other movie stars. I still got the wife I started out with."

"CAIRO'S A GREAT place. I was the only tourist there who never went to see the Sphinx. I've seen Cal Coolidge."

"I AM TICKLED TO
tell all our Dry friends over home that Mrs.
Astor personally is an ardent Prohibitionist;
and when she saw me refuse a drink that was so
strong that the waiter had to wrap it up in a
towel to keep it from blowing up, why, it
seemed to please her very much. Then I pulled
the thing that is an unforgivable sin in England
or Europe—I asked for water. Well, that is just
like asking for Prewar Beer over home. They
have everything else, but nothing disrupts a
well-organized dinner outside America as much
as to have some bonehead ask for a glass of water.
It is just used for raining purposes every day in
England."

This is a snapshot of Will Rogers in a thoroughly characteristic pose and get-up. Between acting scenes on the lot, he would get into the side of his roadster and with his portable typewriter on his knees, would knock off his daily syndicated release.

"BEING GREAT AS President is not a matter of farsightedness; it's just a question of the weather, not only in your own country but in a dozen others. It's the elements that make you great or that break you. If the Lord wants to curse about a dozen other nations that produce the same thing we do, why, then you are in for a renomination. If we are picked out as the goat that year and are to be reprimanded, why, you might be Solomon himself occupying the White House and on March the fourth you would be asked to 'call in a public conveyance and remove any personal belongings that you may have accumulated.' So it's sorter like a World Series—you got to have the breaks.

"You know rain in Iowa, an epidemic of appendicitis among the Bollweevil, or fallen arches on the Chinch Bugs, all play just as big a part in the national career of a man as his executive ability does.

"They say you must have the tide with you to swim the Channel. Well, you certainly have to have the weather with you to keep on being President."

Will Rogers in a pensive moment watching minor actors in a scene from one of his starring vehicles.

Special Cable

CALCOOL, Washhousewhite:

LONDON, May 18.--Nancy Astory
(which is the nom de plume of
Lady Astor) is arriving on your
side soon. She is the best friend
America has here. Please take
care of her. She is the only one
over here that don't throw rocks
at American tourists.

WILLROG.

On British Coffee:

"ENGLAND HAS THE best statesmen and the rottenest coffee of any country in the world.

"Personally, I will be perfectly willing to sign over my share in the debt settlement for just one good cup of coffee. Damn it, we give 'em good tea, and all we demand is reciprocity."

With Speaker Rainey of
the House of Representa-
tives between them, Will
Rogers is shaking hands
with another Will Rogers,
also of Oklahoma, a Con-
gressman.

Observations on the Democratic National Convention, 1932:

"AH! THEY WAS DEM-ocrats today, and we was proud of 'em. They fought, they fit, they split, and adjourned in a dandy wave of dissension. That's the old Democratic spirit. A whole day wasted and nothing done. I tell you, they are getting back to normal. . . . A Democrat never adjourns. He is born, becomes of voting age and starts right in arguing over something, and his first political adjournment is his date with the undertaker. . . . Chicago is on her very good behavior. There hasn't been a soul shot. No devilment of any kind. It's been a fine convention, nobody nominated, nothing done. But what difference does it make? After all, we are just Democrats."

Rogers addressed the convention, saying in part:

"All I have to do is stand up here and play the fool till the Democratic party agrees upon a platform, and that means I'll be here from now on. As soon as enough members of the committee get sober we probably will hear the Prohibition plank. . . . I don't see how you could pick a man weak enough to lose. If he lives until November, he'll be in. . . ."

Of the Democrat's repeal plank:

"Did the Democrats go wet? No, they just laid right down and wallowed in it. They left all their clothes on the bank and dived in without even a bathing-suit. They are wetter than an organdie dress at a rainy-day picnic. The plank was made from cork and nailed together with a sponge."

Will Rogers in his very
earliest motion picture
days when he was making
silent shorts.

Will Rogers

At the 1932 Republican National Convention:

"AND SO TODAY, during a lull when the Ohio pall-bearers wasn't singing the blues, why, Bert [Bert Snell] jumped to the microphone and showed those eleven hundred Republican postmasters seated as delegates that Judas Iscariot was the first Democratic floor leader and Al Capone was one of the last. Then he said that while our Saviour had rescued the world in Biblical times from the Democrats, masquerading as the Medes and Persians, that Herbert Hoover was the modern Saviour. In fact he kinder give the engineer the edge over the carpenter. . . . Our Joe Scott from California, an orator from a crop of orators, nominated Mr. Hoover. And Joe nominated him, he didn't just put his name up; he *said* something. He is the triple-tongued elocution hound of our own Hollywood. Joe not only nominated Hoover

[112]

but invited everybody to the Olympic Games, not even Democrats barred. Joe took up the hardships of maternity in the early days when mothers had no drugstores and a scarcity of clergymen, and showed that under the guidance of Herbert Hoover all those little difficulties had been rectified. He insinuated that under Democrat Federal control motherhood would again become a burden . . ."

As a radio commentator, Will Rogers was tops, attracting the largest air audiences with his quaint quips.

Will Rogers

Rogers' views on art:

"IN THE FIRST PLACE, I don't care anything about oil paintings. Ever since I struck a dry hole near the old home ranch in Rogers County, Oklahoma, I have hated oil, in the raw, and all its subsidiaries. You can even color it up and it don't mean anything to me. I don't want to see a lot of old pictures. If I wanted to see old pictures I would get D. W. Griffith to revive the 'Birth of a Nation.' That's the best old picture there is. . . . But this thinking everything is good because it is old is apple sauce. . . . We know about nine-tenths of the stuff going on under the guise of Art is the banana oil. They call it Art to get to take off the clothes. . . . When you ain't nothing else, you are an artist. It's the one thing you can claim to be and nobody can prove you ain't. . . .

"The whole of Rome seems to have been built, painted and decorated by one man; that was Michelangelo. If you took everything out of Rome that was supposed to have been done by Michelangelo, Rome would be as bare of art as Los Angeles."

It was Will Rogers' pet boast that he never owned a dress suit, but this is one instance where he had to wear one in a picture.

"I DIDENT KNOW BEfore I got there, and they told me, that Rome had Senators. Now I know why it declined.

"They used to have a wall around the city but the people got to climbing over it so much they just sorter neglected it and let it run down. It got so the wall wouldent keep the people from getting out. They would climb over and go off some other place. You can't keep people in a place with a wall. . . . Look at Sing Sing. They got a better wall than Rome even thought they had, and still very few stay there. . . . Walls are all right to put your back to if somebody is fighting you; it keeps you from backing any further away from them, and sometimes makes you fight when if it wasent for the wall you would keep backing."

Of the gladiators:

"A FELLOW WAS A gladiator as long as he remained alive—that's what made him glad. Saturday night was always rather a ticklish time in the life of a gladiator, for that is when they generally announced the entries for the bull-dogging contest with the lions for the following day. If you defeated your lion you were allowed to be glad for another week. . . . These Romans loved blood. . . . A Roman was never so happy as when he saw somebody bleeding. That was his sense of humor, just like ours is. If we see a fellow slip and fall and maybe break his leg, why, that's a yell to us. . . . Well, that's the way the Romans were. Where we like to see you lose your hat they loved to see you leave a right arm and a left leg in the possession of a tiger and then try to make the fence unaided. . . . And there was none of this Dempsey stuff of four years between combats, no dickering over terms. The gate receipts went to the Emperor and you went to the cemetery."

Arriving in Chicago in 1932 for the Republican National Convention. He never missed a presidential conclave of either principal party during the last twenty years of his life.

"WHEN I DIE MY EPI-taph, or whatever you call those signs on grave-stones, is going to read, 'I joked about every prominent man of my time, but I never met a man I didn't like.'

"I am proud of that. I can hardly wait to die so it can be carved.

"And when you come around to my grave you'll probably find me sitting there proudly reading it."